MOTORSPORTS

MONSTER TRUCKS

by Alissa Thielges

body

ramp

Look for these words and pictures as you read.

tire

backflip

A monster truck jumps.
It does cool stunts at events.

A monster truck is big.

It is tough.

It has a lot of power.

PLAY'N FOR KEEPS
DEPENDABLE
HEATING & AIR CONDITIONING
XO-FAB.COM
Tony's
PORTERFIELD
916-662-1945

See the body?
Each truck is different.
This one looks like a dog.

body

MONSTER MUTT
Candice Jolly
BKT
BKT
BKT
BKT

See the ramp?
Monster trucks jump off it.
They race each other.

MONSTER JAM
MONSTER JAM
TEAM HOT WHEELS
GLOBAL ARABSCAN

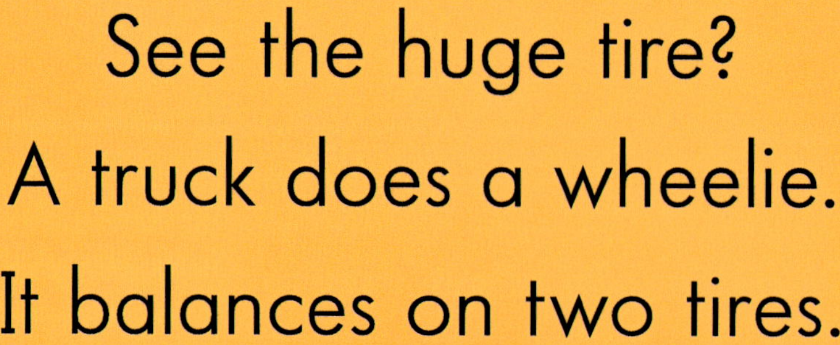

See the huge tire?
A truck does a wheelie.
It balances on two tires.

tire

BKT
THE AMAZING SPIDER-MAN
SPIDER-MAN

GAMEX
GAMEX GAMACHE.NET
GAMACHE

See the backflip?
It flips in a complete circle.
What a cool trick!

A truck jumps high in the air.
Look at it go!

Did you find?

body

ramp

tire

backflip

Spot is published by Amicus Learning, an imprint of Amicus
P.O. Box 227, Mankato, MN 56002
www.amicuspublishing.us

Library of Congress Cataloging-in-Publication Data
Names: Thielges, Alissa, 1995- author.
Title: Monster trucks / by Alissa Thielges.
Description: Mankato, MN : Amicus Learning, [2026] |
   Series: Spot motorsports | Audience: Ages 4–7 |
   Audience: Grades K–1 | Summary: "Monster trucks
   are huge trucks with giant tires. They perform stunts
   at events. This search-and-find book reinforces new
   vocabulary words with simple facts and compelling
   photographs to teach kindergarten readers
   about motorsports"– Provided by publisher.
Identifiers: LCCN 2024050081 (print) | LCCN 2024050082
   (ebook) | ISBN 9798892004855 (library binding) |
   ISBN 9798892005395 (paperback) |
   ISBN 9798892005937 (ebook)
Subjects: LCSH: Monster trucks—Juvenile literature. |
   Monster trucks—Competitions—Juvenile
   literature. | CYAC: Monster trucks.
Classification: LCC TL230.5.M58 T54 2026 (print) |
   LCC TL230.5.M58 (ebook) | DDC
   629.223/2—dc23/eng/20241219
LC record available at https://lccn.loc.gov/2024050081
LC ebook record available at https://lccn.loc.
   gov/2024050082

Ana Brauer, editor
Deb Miner, series designer
Sara Hood, book designer
 and photo researcher

Photos by Alamy Stock Photo/Jane
Barker, 1, kevin cable, 3, Lee Brown,
12–13; Dreamstime/Ahriam12, 14,
Alterfalter, cover; Getty Images/
FAYEZ NURELDINE, 8–9, Waleed
Zein/Anadolu, 10–11; Shutterstock/
BW Press, 6–7, luckyluke007, 4–5